The man with the rubber hose in his nose.

by Anita Weaver

Anita Weaver

Sydney Burns

Dedicated to

Richard "Buster" Lemmon,

a fun Grandpa

and a wonderful friend

ACKNOWLEDGMENTS

I want to give my heartfelt thanks --

To nine-year-old Lacey Jean Chittum for creating the delightful font for the cover

To Laura Gray, my daughter, for her creative advice, love and encouragement.

To my family and friends who have patiently listened to me talk about my writing endeavor and waited for the day they could finally see the finished product.

To Washington High School's class of 1968, who have reconnected, bonded, prayed for and supported each other in recent years. I am blessed to call you my friends.

And most importantly, Thank you, Lord, for enabling me to complete this project. I am amazed what You are able to do through me.

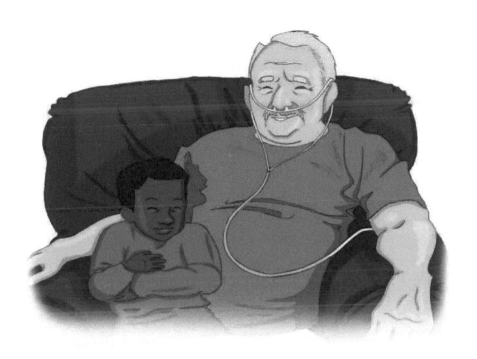

I know a man that looks kind of weird

He has a rubber hose coming out of his nose

But there's no reason he should be feared

He still has 10 fingers and still has 10 toes.

The hose helps him breathe

So we can play and have fun

I laugh at his false teeth

He fakes being mad then I run.

He once was a sailor

And played in a band

He was always a joker

Just so you understand

Then as a policeman he jailed

The guys who do really bad things

He was strong and brave

Told me 'bout undercover stings.

Now he spends time with me

And he tries to be tough

But when I'm still going

He's had enough.

We dress up as sheriffs

The law in the territory

We dress up as boxers

And "Mad Dog" is what he calls me

When I've clearly won

And "Too Old Lemmon's" defeated

Then the Old Man yells

"That punk cheated!"

He took me to Bermuda

Where his ship once sailed

The seas were so rough

We hung onto the rails.

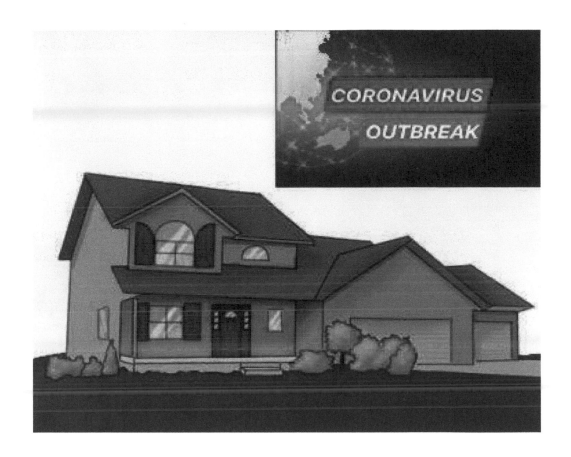

I stayed at his house

When the whole country stood still

Each day was fun

Our pretending seemed real.

I still did my schoolwork

On computer each day

But when it was over

We found new ways to play

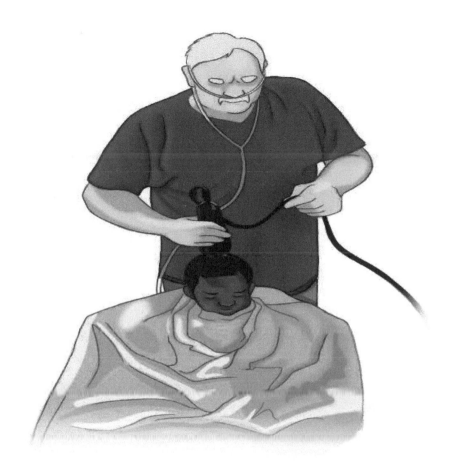

I fake played the piano

He recorded it to share

Then he took out some clippers

And trimmed up my hair.

There's a swing in his yard

And also garden hoses

Cause in his spare time

He grows beautiful roses.

You see he's my Grandpa

During these times we enjoy

The hose disappears

And he calls me "City Boy".